books by
BOXER
www.booksbyboxer.com

Bee Three Books

Bee Three Publishing is an imprint of Books By Boxer
Published by
Books By Boxer, Leeds, LS13 4BS UK
Books by Boxer (EU), Dublin D02 P593 IRELAND
© Books By Boxer 2023
All Rights Reserved
ISBN: 9781915410177
MADE IN MALTA

MIX
Paper from
responsible sources
FSC® C022612

This book is produced from responsibly sourced paper to ensure forest management

GOLDEN GATE FIZZ

Life is short, the world is wide!
Go have a cocktail!

INGREDIENTS (ML/OZ.)

45ml | 1 ½ oz. Amaro
15ml | ½ oz. Grapefruit juice
60ml | 2 oz. Sparkling wine
Grapefruit zest twist for garnish

HOW TO PREPARE:

1. Using a coupe glass first add your amaro liqueur and grapefruit juice.

2. Slowly pour your sparkling wine gently down the side of the glass or over the back of a spoon to avoid bubbles.

3. Garnish your glass with your grapefruit twist.

FRENCH 75

This light and classic drink is an easy-pleaser sure to make you feel fancy!

INGREDIENTS (ML/OZ.)

30ml | 1 oz. Gin
15ml | ½ oz. Lemon juice
15ml | ½ oz. Simple syrup
90ml | 3 oz. Champagne (or any sparkling white wine)
Lemon rind for garnish

HOW TO PREPARE:

1. Pour the gin, lemon juice and simple syrup into your shaker and shake with ice.

2. Strain mixture into a champagne flute.

3. Top with champagne, before giving it a final stir and garnishing it with a twist of lemon rind!

BLACKBERRY MOJITO

Sometimes all you need is a mojito.

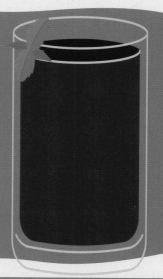

TO MAKE YOUR SIMPLE SYRUP SLOWLY DISSOLVE EQUAL PARTS WATER AND SUGAR OVER A LOW HEAT. LEAVE TO COOL AND YOUR SYRUP IS READY TO USE. THIS CAN BE MADE IN BULK AND KEPT IN THE FRIDGE FOR FUTURE COCKTAILS!

INGREDIENTS (ML/OZ.)

60ml | 2 oz. White rum
20ml | ¾ oz. Lime juice
20ml | ¾ oz. Simple syrup
Soda water to fill glass
8 mint leaves
4-5 muddled blackberries

HOW TO PREPARE:

1. Muddle (roughly crush) the blackberries and mint leaves with the rum, lime juice and simple syrup and shake in your cocktail shaker.

2. Strain the shaken ingredients into a glass with ice and top with soda water.

3. Garnish with additional mint leaves and blackberries.

DEVIL'S MARGARITA

Red wine + margarita?
Please don't call the police—trust us!
This is a great combination that adds a depth to a
firm favorite!

INGREDIENTS (ML/OZ.)

45ml | 1 ½ oz. Blanco tequila
30ml | 1 oz. Lime juice
20ml | ¾ oz. Simple syrup
15ml | ½ oz. Red wine
Lime slice for garnish

HOW TO PREPARE:

1. Add the tequila, lime juice and syrup in an ice-filled cocktail shaker and shake vigorously for 30 seconds, or until chilled!

2. Strain into a margarita glass.

3. Float the red wine on top (slowly pour over the back of a bar spoon to help the wine pool on the top!)

4. Garnish with a lime wheel.

BEE'S KNEES

Made with sweet honey and tart lemon, this tempting cocktail really is the bee's knees!

INGREDIENTS (ML/OZ.)

FOR THE HONEY SYRUP
100ml | ½ cup. Honey
3 tbsp Water

FOR THE COCKTAIL
60ml | 2 oz. Gin
30ml | 1 oz. Fresh lemon juice
15ml | ½ oz. Honey syrup

HOW TO PREPARE:

1. In a saucepan, add honey and water and simmer until the honey has dissolved.

2. Allow the mixture to cool and then strain.

3. Fill a cocktail shaker with ice and add your newly made syrup, lemon juice and gin. Shake well.

4. Strain the cocktail into a martini glass!

HUGO SPRITZ

Don't like Aperol, but want to be a spritz person? This is the perfect summery drink so you don't feel left behind!

INGREDIENTS (ML/OZ.)

30ml | 1 oz. Elderflower syrup
30ml | 1 oz. Soda water
15ml | ½ oz. Gin
15ml | ½ oz. Lime juice
Prosecco (to top)
2 sprigs mint
1 lime slice

HOW TO PREPARE:

1. Place the syrup, gin, lime and 1 mint sprig into a shaker and muddle lightly.

2. Pour over an ice filled red wine glass, add soda water and then top with prosecco.

3. Serve with a sprig of mint and a slice of lime.

4. Sit in the sunshine and enjoy!

1870 SOUR

A variation on a whiskey sour, this sweet, earthy drink could be perfect for those who want to like whiskey ... but just need a bit of getting used to it!

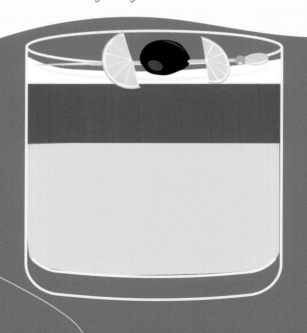

INGREDIENTS (ML/OZ.)

60ml | 2 oz. Tennessee whiskey
30ml | 1 oz. Lemon juice
15ml | ½ oz. Maple syrup
30ml | 1 oz. Zinfandel wine
1 tsp Blueberry jam
1 egg white

HOW TO PREPARE:

1. Add the whiskey, lemon juice, maple syrup, egg white and jam into a shaker – shake for 20 seconds.

2. Add ice to the shaker and shake until cold.

3. Pour into rocks glass.

4. Gently top with wine by pouring over the back of a spoon!

FROZEN DARK & STORMY

This spiced cocktail with a twist is the slushie you've always needed!

INGREDIENTS (ML/OZ.)

120ml | 4 oz. Ginger beer
60ml | 2 oz. Dark rum
1 tbsp. Freshly grated ginger
Juice squeezed from 1 lime
1 lime slice (to garnish)

HOW TO PREPARE:

1. In a blender, blend lime juice, fresh ginger, ginger beer and ice.

2. Pour into a highball glass and pour the rum on top.

3. Garnish with lime and get sipping!

MINT JULEP

Why limit happy to an hour?

INGREDIENTS (ML/OZ.)

60ml | 2 oz. Bourbon
20ml | ¾ oz. Simple syrup
8 mint leaves

HOW TO PREPARE:

1. In your shaker muddle (roughly crush) together the bourbon, sugar syrup and mint leaves.

2. After adding crushed ice to your shaker, gently stir until your drink feels adequately chilled.

3. Strain into your coupe glass, garnish with more mint and serve.

POMEGRANATE & ROSE FIZZ

Delicate, light and floral, this cocktail celebrates love & femininity.

INGREDIENTS (ML/OZ.)

60ml | 2 oz. Prosecco
15ml | ½ oz. Soda water
Juice and seeds of ¼ of a pomegranate
1 tsp Rose water
Garnish with fresh strawberries

HOW TO PREPARE:

1. Allow your prosecco and soda water time to chill before preparing.

2. Combine pomegranate and the rosewater in your flute.

3. Gently pour the chilled prosecco and soda water into your flute.

4. Garnish with the fresh strawberries, stir & enjoy.

RUM RUNNER

Deliciously balancing rum with fruity liqueurs and fresh juice, this cocktail was a classic at a speak-easy bar during prohibition times.

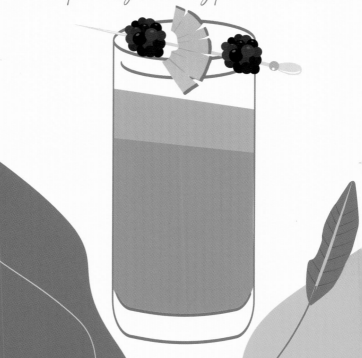

INGREDIENTS (ML/OZ.)

30ml | 1 oz. Dark rum
30ml | 1 oz. White rum
30ml | 1 oz. Banana liqueur
30ml | 1 oz. Blackberry liqueur
45ml | 1 ½ oz. Pineapple juice
15ml | ½ oz. Lime juice
Splash of grenadine
Pineapple wedge & blackberries for garnish

HOW TO PREPARE:

1. Add 4 or 5 cubes of ice to a shaker and then add all of your liquids (rum, liqueurs, juices and grenadine).

2. Shake until chilled and pour into a highball glass with crushed ice.

3. Give your cocktail a tropical finish with a garnish of fresh pineapple and blackberries.

PEACH MARGARITA

The only thing better than one margarita is two margaritas! Enjoy this sweet peach twist on a classic.

INGREDIENTS (ML/OZ.)

60ml | 2 oz. Blanco tequila
15ml | ½ oz. Peach schnapps
30ml | 1 oz. Lime juice
1 small peach, peeled and roughly chopped
Tajín for rim (chili salt works well)
Peach slices for garnish (alternatively use lime wheels)

HOW TO PREPARE:

1. Add chopped peach into a food processor or blender. Blend completely until it forms a liquid consistency. Rub the outer rim of a glass with a lime and rim with tajín.

2. In a cocktail shaker combine tequila, peach schnapps, lime juice and 1 oz. of peach puree. Add ice and shake vigorously.

3. Strain into margarita glass and top with ice. Garnish with a peach slice or lime wedge.

DIRTY MARTINI

Perfect for a savory sip on a cosy evening!

TOP TIP: FEEL FREE TO ADD MORE OLIVE BRINE IF YOU LIKE YOUR MARTINI EXTRA SAVORY!

INGREDIENTS (ML/OZ.)

15 ml / ½ oz. Olive brine
75 ml / 2 ½. Dry gin (this can be swapped
with vodka if you're not a gin fan!)
15 ml / ½ oz. Dry vermouth
3 or 4 Ice cubes (and more for cooling the
glass)
3 green olives, pitted

HOW TO PREPARE:

1. Fill your martini glass up with ice.

2. Skewer your olives on a cocktail stick.

3. Pour all ingredients into your cocktail
shaker.

4. For a silkier, richer cocktail, stir the
ingredients gently! For a frothier, more
diluted drink, shake the shaker for 5-10
seconds!

5. Empty the ice out of the glass and
strain your martini.

6. Garnish with your olives and enjoy!

PINK GRAPEFRUIT SPRITZ

This is your new drink of the summer
(sorry other spritzes–it's a tough fight!)

INGREDIENTS (ML/OZ.)

75ml | 2 ½ oz. Rose vermouth
30ml | 1 oz. Aperol
90ml | 3 oz. Pink grapefruit soda
Grapefruit and mint for garnish

HOW TO PREPARE:

1. Pour all ingredients in a red wine glass filled with ice.

2. Gently combine and top with a grapefruit slice and a sprig of mint.

3. Enjoy!

HINT: ADD AN EXTRA SHOT OF GIN OR VODKA (WHAT-EVER YOUR PREFERENCE) FOR A PUNCHIER HIT!

EL DURAZNO

In this cocktail, the classic pairing of tequila and citrus gets a fun and fruity makeover!

INGREDIENTS (ML/OZ.)

20ml | ¾ oz. Lime juice
20ml | ¾ oz. Simple syrup
15ml | ½ oz. Orange juice
30ml | 1 oz. White peach puree
20ml | ¾ oz. Peach liqueur
40ml | 1 ¼ oz. Blanco tequila
Salt (for rim)

HOW TO PREPARE:

1. Combine all ingredients in your cocktail shaker with ice, and shake vigorously for 30 seconds.

2. Leave to stand, and begin rim your rocks glass with fresh lime around and gently rub salt on the rim of the glass.

3. Pour in your cocktail and enjoy!

MORE SUPREME

Halfway between a daiquiri and a negroni, this rich, bitter and almost savory drink is the perfect aperetivo!

INGREDIENTS (ML/OZ.)

45ml | 1 ½ oz. Dark rum
20ml | ¾ oz. Lime juice
15ml | ½ oz. Simple syrup
7.5ml | ¼ oz. Campari

HOW TO PREPARE:

1. Combine all ingredients (apart from the Campari) into a cocktail shaker and shake lightly with ice for 30 seconds.

2. Strain into a chilled coupe glass.

3. Slowly pour the Campari against the inside of the glass.

4. Garnish with freshly cracked black pepper!

SPARKLING SAGE

Herbaceous and light, this sweet-yet-savory tipple is a fun and fancy way to spruce up your standard bubbles!

INGREDIENTS (ML/OZ.)

45ml | 1 ½ oz. Dark rum
20ml | ¾ oz. Honey syrup
(can be swapped with 2 tsp honey)
15ml | ½ oz. Lime juice
65ml | 2 ¼ oz. Dry sparkling wine
3 sage leaves

HOW TO PREPARE:

1. Add rum, lime, honey syrup, sage and ice into a shaker and shake for 30 seconds.

2. Strain into a champagne glass and top with sparkling wine.

3. Garnish with a sage leaf and some lemon!

GINGER WHISKEY SPRITZ

Maybe it's the alcohol talking but I want another cocktail!

INGREDIENTS (ML/OZ.)

30ml | 1 oz. Whiskey
60ml | 2 oz. Ginger ale
90ml | 3 oz. Sparkling apple juice
Lemon wedge for garnish
Ice

HOW TO PREPARE:

1. Fill a highball glass with ice and leave to chill for 3 minutes.

2. Add your whiskey of choice to the glass, pouring over the ginger ale.

3. Gently squeeze the wedge of lemon into the glass, dropping into the glass after to use as a garnish.

4. Top your glass with sparkling apple juice and stir before finally serving.

BITTER QUEEN

Calling all Campari lovers! This cocktail is perfect after a homemade Italian meal!

INGREDIENTS (ML/OZ.)

45ml | 1 ½ oz. Vodka
30ml | 1 oz. Campari
60ml | 2 oz. Orange juice
30ml | 1 oz. Limoncello
1 Lime slice (for garnish)

HOW TO PREPARE:

1. Add vodka, Campari and limoncello to a shaker and fill with ice.

2. Shake vigorously for 30 seconds, or until shaker has cooled.

3. Strain into a chilled martini glass, and top with orange juice.

4. Garnish with the slice of lime – enjoy!

ROSÉ SPRITZ

Stop and smell the rose.

INGREDIENTS (ML/OZ.)

60ml | 2 oz. Rosé wine
60ml | 2 oz. Sparkling wine
30ml | 1 oz. Aperol
Grapefruit wedge for garnish

HOW TO PREPARE:

1. Add ice to a red wine glass and pour over your Aperol, rosé & sparkling wine.

2. Squeeze your grapefruit wedge into the glass and gently drop in to use as garnish.

3. Stir before serving.

PINK NEGRONI

Put a pink twist on this classic cocktail, garnish with pink grapefruit and a basil leaf to fabulously compliment the pink gin, rose vermouth & Aperol.

INGREDIENTS (ML/OZ.)

30ml | 1 oz. Pink gin
30ml | 1 oz. Rose vermouth
15ml | ½ oz. Aperol
Few cubes of ice
Wedge of pink grapefruit and a
basil leaf, to garnish

HOW TO PREPARE:

1. Add plenty of ice to a rocks glass.

2. Combine the pink gin, vermouth and
Aperol in the glass.

3. Stir until the outside of the glass feels
cold.

4. Garnish with a wedge of pink grapefruit
and a basil leaf and serve!

VENETIAN SUNRISE

Cocktails: because no great story ever started with someone eating a salad.

INGREDIENTS (ML/OZ.)

30ml | 1 oz. Aperol
30ml | 1 oz. White rum
30ml | 1 oz. Pineapple juice
15ml | ½ oz. Simple syrup
15ml | ½ oz. Rosé wine
1 tsp Vanilla syrup
1 tsp Orange bitters
Dried orange slices for garnish

HOW TO PREPARE:

1. Add all of your ingredients to a cocktail shaker with ice.

2. Shake mixture well until cold. Then pour your shaken mixture into a chilled coupe glass.

3. Garnish with the orange slice, serve and enjoy!

SEX ON THE BEACH

Add some zing to your sip with this delicious tropical cocktail!

INGREDIENTS (ML/OZ.)

40ml | 1 ½ oz. Vodka
15ml | ½ oz. Crème de Cassis
20ml | ¾ oz. Peach schnapps
60ml | 2 oz. Orange juice
60ml | 2 oz. Cranberry juice
Orange slice (to garnish)
Maraschino cherry (to garnish)

HOW TO PREPARE:

1. Pour all the ingredients into an ice-filled cocktail shaker, and shake it up!

2. Pack ice into a highball glass and strain the cocktail into it.

3. Garnish with a maraschino cherry and orange slice!

THE LAST WORD

Have the last word in any disagreement by serving up this marvellous cocktail!

INGREDIENTS (ML/OZ.)

20ml | ¾ oz. Gin
20ml | ¾ oz. Fresh lime juice
20ml | ¾ oz. Maraschino liqueur
20ml | ¾ oz. Green Chartreuse
Brandied cherry (to garnish)

HOW TO PREPARE:

1. Add all the ingredients into a cocktail shaker.

2. Fill the shaker with ice, and shake well for 10 seconds.

3. Strain the cocktail into your favourite martini glass, and drink up!

STRAWBERRY PROSECCO SMASH

This dreamy cocktail is strawberries and cream in liquid form—with a fizz!

INGREDIENTS (ML/OZ.)

30ml | 1 oz. Cream of coconut
½ tsp Honey
½ Lemon, squeezed
Prosecco (to fill)
3 strawberries, diced

HOW TO PREPARE:

1. Shake strawberries in a cocktail shaker until their juices release.

2. Squeeze the lemon, and add honey and cream of coconut into the shaker with ice.

3. Shake vigorously for ten seconds and pour into your favourite rocks glass.

4. Top with prosecco and enjoy!

FRENCH PEARL

Be brave with this herbaceous and simple sipper!

INGREDIENTS (ML/OZ.)

60ml | 2 oz. Gin
7.5ml | ¼ oz. Pastis (anise liqueur)
20ml | ¾ oz. Lime juice
20ml | ¾ oz. Simple syrup
6 mint sprigs

HOW TO PREPARE:

1. In a shaker, add the lime juice, syrup and mint, and muddle it.

2. Add the gin, pastis and ice, and shake until completely chilled.

3. Strain into a coupe glass, and garnish with 2 mint leaves and a slice of lime.

VIEW FROM THE STARS

This quick and easy two step cocktail is sure to taste out of this world!

INGREDIENTS (ML/OZ.)

30ml | 1 oz. Gin
15ml | ½ oz. Blueberry lavender syrup
20ml | ¾ oz. Lemon juice
Prosecco
Ice

HOW TO PREPARE:

1. Add gin, lemon juice, and blueberry lavender syrup into a cocktail shaker and shake well.

2. Pour into a champagne flute and top with prosecco!

LEMON DROP MARTINI

This tarty lemon cocktail is perfect for lounging in the sun on a hot day!

INGREDIENTS (ML/OZ.)

40ml | 1 ½ oz. Vodka
20ml | ¾ oz. Cointreau
20ml | ¾ oz. Lemon juice
1 tsp Simple syrup
Lemon slice to garnish

HOW TO PREPARE:

1. Garnish the glass with a rim of sugar.

2. Add all of the ingredients into a cocktail shaker then strain over ice into your martini glass.

3. Serve with a slice of lemon.

APEROL SPRITZ

A taste of summer, sit back and relax in the sun with this refreshing spritz cocktail.

INGREDIENTS (ML/OZ.)

60ml | 2 oz. Aperol
60ml | 2 oz. Prosecco
30ml | 1 oz. Soda water
Garnish with an orange slice
Ice

HOW TO PREPARE:

1. Add plenty of ice to a red wine glass.

2. Into your glass combine the Aperol and prosecco, and top with the soda water.

3. Garnish with an orange slice.

WITCH'S BREW

This earthy, smoky and sour cocktail is the perfect drink to welcome in those darker nights!

INGREDIENTS (ML/OZ.)

60ml | 2 oz. Whiskey
15ml | ½ oz. Sherry
30ml | 1 oz. Lemon juice
15ml | ½ oz. Simple syrup
15ml | ½ oz. Beetroot juice
Cherry (to garnish)

HOW TO PREPARE:

1. Add all ingredients (apart from the beetroot juice) into a cocktail shaker with ice, and shake until cooled.

2. Strain into a rocks glass over ice.

3. Top up ith your beetroot juice and cherry, enjoy!

VIOLET COSMO

This refreshing cosmo with a twist is the perfect tipple when enjoying the sunshine!

INGREDIENTS (ML/OZ.)

20ml | ¾ oz. Lemon juice
30ml | 1 oz. White cranberry juice
15ml | ½ oz. Orange-flavored liqueur
7.5ml | ¼ oz. Crème de Cassis
7.5ml | ¼ oz. Crème de Violette
45ml | 1 ½ oz. Citrus-flavored vodka
Blackberry (to garnish)

HOW TO PREPARE:

1. Add all your ingredients into a cocktail shaker, add ice and shake it up!

2. Strain into a chilled martini glass.

3. Garnish with a lavender sprig, and sip up!

TROPICAL PALOMA

This tiki take on a classic is great for bringing some summer into your life!

INGREDIENTS (ML/OZ.)

45ml / 1 ½ oz. Blanco tequila
30 ml / 1 oz. Grapefruit juice
20ml / ¾ oz. Lime juice
15ml / ½ oz. Curacao
Grapefruit wedge
Ice

HOW TO PREPARE:

1. Add all juices and alcohol to your shaker.

2. Add ice and shake.

3. Strain into a glass over ice.

4. Garnish with your grapefruit wedge, and enjoy!

NEGRONI SBAGLIATO

This refreshing cosmo with a twist is the perfect tipple when enjoying the sunshine!

INGREDIENTS (ML/OZ.)

30ml | 1 oz. Campari
30ml | 1 oz. Sweet vermouth
Prosecco (enough to top your glass of choice)
Dried orange slice for garnish

HOW TO PREPARE:

1. First pour your Campari and sweet vermouth over ice.

2. Gently pour your prosecco down the edge of the glass to avoid bubbles.

3. Use a spoon or a stirrer to mix the contents together — topping up with more prosecco if required and garnish your glass with the dried orange slice.

NEW YORK SOUR

Feel the buzz of the big city with this sophisticated classic.

INGREDIENTS (ML/OZ.)

60ml | 2 oz. Bourbon
30ml | 1 oz. Lemon juice
15ml | ½ oz. Maple syrup
30ml | 1 oz. Red wine
Lemon twist for garnish

HOW TO PREPARE:

1. Into your cocktail shaker add the bourbon, lemon juice and maple syrup to your cocktail shaker with 3-4 ice cubes. Shake vigorously until well combined and chilled.

2. Fill your glass with ice and pour your shaken mixture into the glass.

3. Using the back of a spoon gently pour the red wine onto the surface of the drink, you should see a red layer form at the top of your drink.

4. Garnish with the lemon twist and serve.

PIÑA COLADA SANGRIA

Set sail and sip yourself onto a tropical beach with this yummy pitcher!

INGREDIENTS (ML/OZ.)

1 bottle of White wine
350ml | 1 ½ cups Pineapple juice
230ml | 1 cup Seltzer
210g | 1 cups Chopped pineapple
115 | ½ cups Coconut rum
65ml | ¼ cups Maraschino cherries

HOW TO PREPARE:

1. In a pitcher, add the wine, pineapple juice, seltzer, coconut rum, pineapple and cherries.

2. Stir and refrigerate until cool.

3. Pour into your favourite cocktail glass and garnish with a pineapple chunk.

LIMONCELLO SOUR

Citrusy, velvety and light, this summery cocktail is a holiday in a glass!

INGREDIENTS (ML/OZ.)

60ml | 2 oz. Limoncello
30ml | 1 oz. Lemon juice
30ml | 1 oz. Simple syrup
1 Egg white
1 dash Angostura Bitters

HOW TO PREPARE:

1. Pour all ingredients into your shaker.

2. Perform a dry shake (without ice).

3. After 30 seconds, add ice and shake for 1 minute.

4. Strain into a glass, and garnish with lemon rind.

DUCK FART SHOT

This fun, three-tiered cocktail tastes much better than its name gives credit for!

INGREDIENTS (ML/OZ.)

15ml | ½ oz. Coffee liqueur
15ml | ½ oz. Irish cream
15ml | ½ oz. Whiskey

HOW TO PREPARE:

1. Pour the Coffee liqueur into a long shot glass.

2. Carefully add the Baileys, pouring over the back of a spoon.

3. Pour the whiskey over the back of a spoon as before.

VIOLET COSMO

*This refreshing cosmo with a twist is the
perfect tipple when enjoying the sunshine!*

INGREDIENTS (ML/OZ.)

45ml | 1 ½ oz. White rum
7.5ml | ¼ oz. Simple syrup
30ml | ½ oz. Coconut milk
7.5ml | ¼ oz. Crème de cacao
5 Mint leaves
Vanilla soda to fill glass

HOW TO PREPARE:

1. Add the mint leaves to a glass with ice.

2. Pour the rum, simple syrup, coconut milk & crème de cacao to the glass, stir well and then top with the vanilla soda.

3. Garnish with more mint and serve.

BOOZY SHAMROCK SHAKE

Bring out your inner child with this grown-up shamrock shake!

SERVES 4

INGREDIENTS (ML/OZ.)

12 scoops Vanilla ice cream
115ml | ½ cup Creme de menthe
80ml | ⅓ cup Whiskey
80ml | ⅓ cup Baileys
Whipped cream
Sprinkles (to garnish)

HOW TO PREPARE:

1. Add the ice cream, whiskey, Baileys and crème de menthe to a blender and pulse until mixed completely.

2. Pour into your favourite glasses (smoothie glasses work well).

3. Top with whipped cream and top with sprinkles for a hearty dessert!

BUTTERY NIPPLE

A cheeky shot to celebrate nipples in every form, the perfect party starter.

INGREDIENTS (ML/OZ.)

15ml | ½ oz. Irish cream
30ml | 1 oz. Butterscotch schnapps
Drop of grenadine

HOW TO PREPARE:

1. Chill your shot glass for a short time before serving.

2. Add your butterscotch schnapps to your chilled shot glass.

3. Using the back of the spoon gently pour the Irish cream onto the top of the glass – this should allow it to float on top of the butterscotch schnapps.

4. For a cheeky finish add a drop of grenadine onto the top to finish your nipple!

CHOCOLATE MARTINI

A rich twist on the classic martini, perfect for drinkers with a sweet tooth. This Chocolate Martini works best as an after dinner treat.

INGREDIENTS (ML/OZ.)

60ml | 2 oz. Chocolate liqueur
60ml | 2 oz. Irish cream liqueur
60ml | 2 oz. Vodka
Ice
Chocolate syrup
Chocolate shavings to garnish

HOW TO PREPARE:

1. Drizzle chocolate syrup into a martini glass and set aside.

2. Add the chocolate liqueur, Irish cream and vodka to a cocktail shaker with ice. Shake until chilled.

3. Pour and garnish with chocolate shavings for an added sweet treat!

COFFEE & COKE

Bitter yet sweet, this unique blend is sure to tease your taste buds!

INGREDIENTS (ML/OZ.)

30ml | 1 oz. Rye whiskey (or any whiskey of your choice)
10ml | ⅓ oz. Campari
10ml | ⅓ oz. Vermouth
30ml | 1 oz. Espresso
1 dash Chocolate bitters
30ml | 1 oz. Coca-Cola (to top)
1 slice of orange

HOW TO PREPARE:

1. Add all the ingredients except the Coca-Cola into a shaker and shake vigorously for 10 seconds.

2. Strain the cocktail into a rock glass, over ice.

3. Top with Coca-Cola and garnish with an orange slice.

FLOWER POWER SOUR

Vibrant, fruity and tart.
This balanced cocktail is the perfect
springtime drink!

INGREDIENTS (ML/OZ.)

45ml | 1 ½ oz. White rum
30ml | 1 oz. Lemon juice
30ml | ¾ oz. Pineapple juice
35ml | 1 oz. Simple syrup
3-4 dashes Red aromatic bitters
1 Egg white

HOW TO PREPARE:

1. Combine all ingredients into the cocktail shaker and fill with ice.

2. Shake vigorously for 30 seconds, or until all ingredients have chilled.

3. Strain out ice and re-shake for 30 more seconds.

4. Strain into a coupe glass.

5. Garnish with lemon slice (or edible flowers if you really want to impress!)

THE GOLD RUSH

This fresh, sweet and smoky is a perfect (and easy) all-rounder!

INGREDIENTS (ML/OZ.)

60ml / 2 oz. Bourbon
30ml / 1 oz. Lemon juice
15ml / ½ oz. Honey
Ice
Fresh Mint (for garnish)

HOW TO PREPARE:

1. Add all ingredients into a cocktail shaker.

2. Add ice and shake lightly.

3. Pour over a glass with ice and garnish with mint!

STRAWBERRY SWEETHEART MAI TAI

Pretty fly for a Mai Tai.

INGREDIENTS (ML/OZ.)

30ml | 1 oz. White rum
30ml | 1 oz. Dark rum
30ml | 1 oz. Lime juice
15ml | ½ oz. Orgeat syrup (can be
substituted with amaretto)
2 or 3 Chopped strawberries

HOW TO PREPARE:

1. Into your shaker add the white rum, lime juice, orgeat syrup, strawberries and ice.

2. Shake mixture well until cold. Then pour your shaken mixture into a glass of crushed ice.

3. Using the back of the spoon gently pour the dark rum onto the top of the glass – this should allow it to float on top of the shaken mixture.

4. Garnish with another strawberry, serve and enjoy!

MICHELADA

Give your cocktail drinking a kick with
sour and spicy flavours that will have you
coming back for more!

INGREDIENTS (ML/OZ.)

355ml | 12 oz. Light beer
60ml | 2 oz. Fresh lime juice
2 tsp Hot sauce
1 tsp. Salt
1 tsp. Chili powder
Lime wedges
Dash of soy sauce

HOW TO PREPARE:

1. Mix salt and chilli powder together. Wet the rim of a large glass with a lime wedge and dip the rim into the powder.

2. Add lime juice, hot sauce and soy sauce at the bottom of the glass and stir.

3. Fill the glass with ice, and top with beer.

4. Stir gently, and garnish with a lime wedge.

CHOC COOKIE SHOT

Enjoy this sweet tipple on a cosy evening in!

INGREDIENTS (ML/OZ.)

45ml | 1 ½ oz. RumChata (swap for Baileys
if you can't find this!)
30ml | 1 oz. Chocolate vodka
15ml | ½ oz. Chocolate liqueur

HOW TO PREPARE:

1. Pour RumChata into your favourite tall
shot glass.

2. Slowly pour the chocolate vodka over
the back of a spoon into the glass.

3. Carefully pour the chocolate liqueur into
the glass over the back of a spoon.

4. Grab your favourite cookies and enjoy!